MAKO SHARKS

THE SHARK DISCOVERY LIBRARY

Sarah Palmer

Illustrated by Ernest Nicol and Libby Turner

Rourke Enterprises, Inc.
Vero Beach, Florida 32964

© 1988 Rourke Enterprises, Inc.

Library of Congress Cataloging-in-Publication Data

Palmer, Sarah, 1955-
  Mako Sharks

  (The Sharks discovery library)
  Includes index.
  Summary: Describes the appearance, habitat, and
behavior of mako sharks.
    1. Isurus—Juvenile literature. 2. Sharks-Juvenile
literature. [1. Mako sharks. 2. Sharks]
I. Nicol, Ernest et al, ill.
II. Title. III. Series: Palmer,Sarah,1955-
Sharks discovery library.
QL638.95.L3P36   1989   597'.31   88-6429
ISBN 0-86592-458-9

TABLE OF CONTENTS

MAKO SHARKS

Mako sharks belong to the family of mackerel sharks. They are related to the feared great white shark. There are two kinds of mako sharks, the longfin mako and the shortfin mako. Mako sharks are the fastest moving sharks in the world, and one of the fastest fish. They can swim at over 22 miles per hour in short bursts.

Mako sharks can swim very fast

HOW THEY LOOK

Shortfin mako sharks have metallic blue backs with pure white undersides. Longfin makos are much darker, and have a blue-black skin. The largest known longfin mako was 12 feet, 8 inches long. The average size for a female of both **species** is 10 feet. Mako sharks have large **dorsal fins**. Their tail fins are designed for fast swimming: the upper and lower **lobes** are almost the same size.

A longfin and a shortfin mak

WHERE THEY LIVE

Mako sharks live in warm seas. Scientists have found that makos **migrate** to warmer waters in the winter, when the seas where they live cool off. They studied one shortfin mako that swam from the seas near Virginia all the way to the West Indies. That's a distance of 1,690 miles! Longfin makos usually live in deeper waters than shortfin makos.

Shortfin makos live in coral reefs

WHAT THEY EAT

Mako sharks will eat almost any kind of fish. They have been known to eat mackerel, tuna, herring and squid, as well as bigger fish like swordfish and marlins. Makos have dagger-like teeth, which are long and pointed with smooth edges. They use these sharp teeth to spear their **prey**.

Mako sharks sometimes eat swordfish

Shortfin makos can swim long
distances

Mako sharks have
large dorsal fins

SHARK ATTACK!

Shortfin mako sharks are thought to be dangerous. They have been known to attack boats. Boats with white hulls seem to attract attacks by shortfin makos. Makos have been known to attack humans. Scientists warn that they could be deadly. When they are angry, these sharks attack with great strength.

A shortfin mako attacks a white-hulled boat

PREVENTING SHARK ATTACK

Scientists are still looking for the best way to keep sharks away from beaches. Some sharks still get through the nets and fences that are built to keep them away from swimmers. One idea is to use very loud noises to frighten away the sharks. Another system, which has been tested in South Africa, uses cables to produce electrical currents that the sharks will not cross.

A mako breaks through a sha. net

IF A SHARK ATTACKS

A shark attack **victim** will suffer from loss of blood and from shock. The bleeding should be stopped as soon as possible. To bring the injured person out of shock, a greater flow of blood must reach his or her head. The person should be laid on the beach, positioned so the head is lower than the feet. He or she should be wrapped in a blanket until medical aid can arrive. Never try to move an injured person.

A shark victim is carried from the water

BABY MAKO SHARKS

There are three ways in which sharks produce their young. Some sharks lay eggs on the **seabed**, and from these eggs baby sharks hatch. Others produce eggs that they carry inside them until the babies are ready to hatch. Some sharks, like the mako, give birth to live young. Mako sharks normally have four babies each year.

Mako sharks bear live young

FACT FILE

Common Name: Shortfin Mako Shark
Scientific Name: Isurus oxyrinchus
Color: Metallic blue
Average Size: Male   – 7 feet, 10 inches
                   Female – 11 feet
Where They Live: Warm waters, mostly
                   offshore
Danger Level: Dangerous shark

Glossary

dorsal fins (DOR sal FINS) — fins on a shark's back

lobes (LOBES) — the fleshy part of a shark's tail fin

to migrate (MI grate) — to move from one place to another, usually at the same time each year

prey (PREY) — an animal that is hunted for food

seabed (SEA bed) — the floor of the ocean

species (SPE cies) — a scientific term meaning kind or type

victim (VIC tim) — an injured person

INDEX